STEPPING ON
FREEDOM

Cobus Venter

Published by
Brigadiers A&K (Pty) Ltd

Registered Office
PO Box 920
Stellenbosch 7599
South Africa

This work is the personal opinion of the author. It does not reflect on the views or opinion, nor imply endorsement of or by any of the institutions to which the author is attached.

Layout: Carel de Beer

Cover Illustration: Carel de Beer and Marli Fourie

This book is dedicated to three key people. Firstly, my wife who keeps pretending that economics is actually interesting and indulges me in constant debates about our future in this land.

Secondly, to Prof Ben Smit who originally triggered my interest in the subject but perhaps more importantly taught me its relevance in the real world. Few people have positively influenced as many students, myself included, as this soft spoken giant in his field.

Lastly, to Alan Knott-Craig (junior) who stubbornly refuses to become negative about South Africa and does something about it every day by providing free access to proper internet services to all people – not just those who can afford it. Making well informed decisions is a basic requirement for a functioning democracy and the internet is immensely powerful in this regard.

This book is my contribution to the debate. Love it or hate it, no matter, but please think about it!

INDEX

1

SOUTH AFRICA'S ROAD BACK TO A DARKER PAST

The old saying goes that nothing ever changes, but this is simply unacceptable when considering the welfare of real people. South Africa has achieved much since 1994 and things are clearly very different. There is no doubt that the country is a substantially better place to live in for the average citizen in 2015 than was the case in 1994, but there is currently an overwhelming unease among many South Africans who once again fear for the future. The relative collapse of business and consumer confidence to levels last seen just after the transition to democracy has highlighted the fragility of the concept of the rainbow nation. The regular and increasingly aggressive and belligerent and often race based policy discussions around topics such as land reform and nationalisation of assets, has created an uncertain environment for people and companies to operate within.

As a country we must ask ourselves whether we are still on the right path? Will our current trajectory and development plans succeed in lifting our people out of the dire poverty so many experience daily?

Economists typically look at data over a time period and try to understand incentives and causation to various factors shaping daily life. While the discipline has been labelled the "Dismal Science", the central point of economics and the study thereof are ways in which to improve economic outcomes given the resources available. By economic outcomes I mean the general conditions that people live in and work under. There is one major caveat to that statement, namely, that the intention is typically <u>not</u> short term; rather economists try and figure out the best options to **sustainably** and **consistently** improve the outcomes for a society over time.

While many economists will impress you with seemingly very robust and statistically significant explanatory models, it is important to remember that the underlying subject of study is none other than simple humanity and the mortals that make up society as a whole. Reading any newspaper will demonstrate that as people go, South Africa has its fair share of saints, sinners and simple wing nuts. Often the same person can also tick all three boxes depending on timing, incentive and who is taking notes.

Macroeconomics tries to take the individual out of the equation and studies things in their aggregated or final form. For example, the right to private property in a society at large and the benefits flowing are offset against the very real needs of those without property. Over time certain relationships become apparent. There is no shortage of people willing to defend private property rights and why they are so important. Similarly, there is probably no more emotive subject in post-colonial Africa than the question of who owns the land, with many who are willing to simply seize private land in order to redistribute it to others.

Zimbabwe's disastrous land reforms are a great example. Implemented when political patience over the continued ownership and seeming success of white farmers in Zimbabwe reached a limit, the ZANU PF government simply allowed land invasions and seized control of the majority of agricultural land in the country. The original owners mostly received no compensation for the loss of their private property. New owners who, in most cases, were simply well connected supporters of government were appointed. Effectively one set of elites was replaced by another and little was achieved in terms of true access to land for the majority of Zimbabweans. Unfortunately, the impact spread far and wide with agricultural production plummeting, export earnings collapsing and foreign investors withdrawing. Widespread economic collapse followed with rampant and out of control inflation eroding all wealth in the country, except for that already sequestered somewhere safe like Switzerland.

There can be no doubt that many who read the paragraph above will differ greatly with some of the statements and will ardently argue that other factors are to blame.

People (and this mostly includes economists) experience events from their own subjective viewpoint and therefore the interpretation of such events often follow the same subjective lines. Supporters of the land reform policy in Zimbabwe argued that they were being punished for addressing the inequitable distribution of land in the country while opponents stated their belief that the results were inevitable.

Given this subjective view "Truth", as a concept, is seldom absolute.

Because we differ on the definition, the cure then is also not simple to define. Who decides the value of one person's right to property in our example, versus another's desires and needs and which one is more important (where did you think the "dismal" part comes from?). The political system plays out the ever-changing moods of the people and this constantly alters the costs and benefits of pretty much all variables in economics. The market, whether for garden hoses, labour or dating services, continuously adjusts the values that these outcomes imply by changing their absolute and relative prices. If somebody suddenly leaks millions of emails from a website dedicated to cheating, the value of a listing or even the website itself changes instantaneously. What somebody was willing to pay for (a listing), they are suddenly willing to pay for NO listing, all within seconds[1].

But remember that all this is still driven by the same saints, sinners and wing nuts who will do whatever they can to advance their own agendas. This, in turn, changes the incentive structure and it all starts from the beginning yet again. The mere fluidity of human opinion and actions implies that few things are absolute and therefore their values are also constantly changing, requiring a market mechanism to allow for seamless adjustments.

The broad environment within which the market operates is interpreted very differently by very smart economists who study the same things but explain them very differently. Marx, Keynes, Friedman and Hayek, to name but a few of the better known ones from the 20th century, all interpreted things as if they might have happened on different planets but some common ideas did eventually crystallise.

Any decent economist will have the humility to acknowledge that we are not really that good at forecasting the future and that many mistakes are made in the process. However, even taking into account the regular and often spectacular failures in economics, overwhelming proof exists that there are good and bad ways of going about things. The tremendous economic progress made in the 20th century and especially since the Second World War, must be seen as a triumph

---

[1] A tongue in cheek reference to the hacking of dating site Ashley Madison during August 2015.

of rational economics over power politics and the influence of elites. South Africa had its fair share of triumphs and challenges during the 20th century as well, but entered the new millennium in an envious position. The country had seemingly overcome its very deep political differences and was governed by the legitimate outcome of years of constitutional debate to be the darling of positive thought. This was epitomised by the almost universal adoration that Nelson Mandela enjoyed and his new supporters included some of the staunchest opponents from the past.

2

THE SOUTH AFRICAN CASE

The adopting of our new constitution in 1996 laid the legal and moral basis for the new South Africa. It is fair to say that the process leading up to the unbanning of the ANC and the release of Nelson Mandela might have ended very differently had there not been a mutual understanding of the challenges and risks involved in such a massive societal transformation. This paper will not dwell on the massive historical significance of the transition to full multi-party democratic government in South Africa. The memory of the peaceful elections in 1994 is still felt proudly by many if not the vast majority of citizens. The constitution was the culmination of many years of conflict in the country. Fortunately, wise men and women agreed on a way forward that seemingly sought to contain the simmering tensions then prevailing between various groups – both racial and otherwise.

The preamble to the constitution elevated the individual as opposed to the group as the central pillar of society.

We, the people of South Africa, Recognize the injustices of our past; Honour those who suffered for justice and freedom in our land; Respect those who have worked to build and develop our country; and Believe that South Africa belongs to all who live in it, united in our diversity.

We therefore, through our freely elected representatives, adopt this Constitution as the supreme law of the Republic so as to - Heal the divisions of the past and establish a society based on democratic values, social justice and fundamental human rights; Lay the foundations for a democratic and open society in which government is based on the will of the people and every citizen is equally protected by law; Improve the quality of life of all citizens and free the potential of each person; and

Build a united and democratic South Africa able to take its rightful place as a sovereign state in the family of nations. May God protect our people. Nkosi Sikelel' iAfrika. Morena boloka setjhaba sa heso. God seën

Suid-Afrika. God bless South Africa. Mudzimu fhatutshedza Afurika. Hosi katekisa Afrika. [2]

The new government instituted massive change on all spheres of society. Given the broad legitimacy of the process, confidence both domestically and internationally allowed the country to glimpse what success truly meant. Dramatic improvements in most economic indicators followed and comprehensive social reforms and social transfers to the most deserving became signals of the new South African success story. The seemingly impossible started to seem within reach – namely constant improvement in the lives of all without any appreciable negative costs involved. The economy grew strongly, employment and business thrived and due to the progressive nature of our tax system, fiscal income surged. This allowed the new government the space to significantly expand the social welfare net while constantly improving its own finances and pay down debt. In short – Nirvana.

However, change was afoot both politically and economically. Internal factional fighting within the ruling party unseated first the deputy president, then the incumbent president who was in turn replaced by the previous (now-unfired again) deputy president. A very civilised coup, completely bloodless. The peaceful departure of the outgoing president almost solidified the country's reputation as an enlightened modern leader.

But, unfortunately, the change did not end there.

The world lurched into the great financial crisis from which it is still recovering[3]. Our own politics became a mud fight and tax receipts stagnated. Government kept spending, sometimes in a counter cyclical manner which did much to relieve the impact of the financial crisis, but at other times in a seemingly reckless manner. Government,

---

[2] See more at:
   http://www.justice.gov.za/legislation/constitution/preamble. html#sthash.s8CG7FN7.dpuf

[3] The world entered a prolonged period of economic distress from 2008 onwards and is still recovering following the collapse of sub-prime lending in the US.

supposedly due to political rent seeking and keeping constituencies in their camps, started acting like an actor in the economy rather than the umpire. State employees became the recipients of increasing largesse and the government wage bill ballooned by 40% between 2008 and 2015, in real terms, causing much shrugging of shoulders as to the long term sustainability of all this.

Around the same time, subtle but potentially seismic shifts started taking hold within government. While lip service was paid to the very comprehensive and ambitious National Development Plan, the tentacles of control by the state started creeping ever deeper into the economy. Whether the true intention is purely political (i.e. one grouping trying to maintain control at all costs) or social (trying to change the structure of society), the impact is clear for all to see. Increasing government interference with many state owned- or run institutions such as ESKOM, SARS and the SABC coupled to the concept of the developmental state, as espoused by many in government, seem to indicate a more general acceptance that the state will play a firmer role in shaping our futures than the recent past indicated.

Allowing for a subjective, or more honestly perhaps ideological, interpretation of these events indicates that our future economic pathway will increasingly be influenced and directed by state efforts. This state involvement might take the part of active economic agent where the state uses its regulatory powers to further its own goals such as in media coverage[4], or more indirectly by procurement policies and price controls such as scrap metals or minimum prescribed investments for pension funds.

The ideological viewpoint of the participant is also very relevant in the interpretation of events. If your view is that a company that is successful in the manufacturing of a product requires ten workers to function, then imposing a minimum wage will have no effect on employment. Rather, it will enhance the welfare of the workers now enjoying higher wages. If, however, your view is that companies are well informed price takers and exist to maximise profits via least cost

---

[4] The state often accuses the media of having an own agenda and not maintaining neutrality in reporting

production, then it is conceivable that at some labour price point a substitute for physical labour becomes viable. At this point, higher minimum wages might result in job losses as companies automate or import rather than produce locally.

It is probably another uncomfortable thought to those who deem themselves intellectual or original thinkers, but there exists very little truly new or original thought in economics. It is mostly a slow progression of building on an ever-developing and increasing knowledge-base within an imperfect knowledge world.

The most famous saying in economics is probably that of the great John Maynard Keynes who stated:

"The ideas of economists and political philosophers, both when they are right and when they are wrong, are more powerful than is commonly understood. Indeed the world is ruled by little else. Practical men, who believe themselves'to be quite exempt from any intellectual influences, are usually the slaves of some defunct economist." [5]

State interference might also make initial sense and be intuitively welcomed by society at large. Who does not like more equitable coal supply contracts for the power stations? It seems like a good idea to give the smaller coal mines a chance of selling their coal to Eskom, surely? But what if the very size of the coal mine or middleman selling the coal is such that they cannot deliver enough on time at the right station? Is the resulting load-shedding of power not causing much greater harm to the economy than the "good" coming from setting smaller mines up to compete against the big boys? If the intervention includes allowing the small mines to charge higher prices for the coal they do deliver. It also increases the cost of generating the power we all use, which results in Eskom increasing the price of electricity. Higher electricity prices hurt the poor much more than the rich as they spend much more, relative to income, on electricity.

---

[5] Keynes, The General Theory of Employment, Interest and Money. p383

Some form of price control on scrap iron and copper has been bandied about and implemented by the government as a solution to the ever-growing loss of domestic casting capacity[6]. The local foundries find that they cannot compete with cheap imports from places like China, due to their high input costs. Obviously scrap metal is a large part of this cost so logically it must follow that if we have cheaper scrap we would be able to compete more effectively. "We all know it is stolen anyway" so who cares about the price? Well the several hundreds of thousands of incredibly poor people who collect scrap for a living certainly care. Yes, some of them might be criminals, but do you really think all of them are? Criminals will simply steal more to make up the difference, but for the poor that go around with their trolleys, even R10 makes a difference, yet the DTI thinks it is acceptable to decide on their behalf that the well-being of a foundry is more important than feeding their kids? Emotive sure, but what about the impact of higher electricity costs on the foundries? Which is more important as variable? Scrap metals follow international prices and pricing goes up AND down, yet electricity constantly increases in price?

The point is that there are so many variables to consider, that intervening in the price of one has absolutely no guarantee of success, as has unfortunately been shown in the case of scrap metal, with the domestic metal manufacturing industry still under massive and increasing pressure in spite of the interventions. Unfortunately they did not help the metal manufacturing industries AND they caused additional hardship to others. Bad medicine that did not work...

The dismal science, unfortunately, often points to uncomfortable aspects of policies that are often not obvious at first glance.

---

[6] See **www.econex.co.za** for various research notes on the impacts of domestic price controls on scrap metals.

3

SHOULD YOU CARE AND WHO IS THIS HAYEK CHAP?

Why write yet another piece critical of current economic policy when there is already so much written? This paper is by no means meant as criticism of government, as government is hardly a coherent concept.

This paper is not about economics in isolation either. Rather it aims to inform the reader about the current South African situation from a historical, political and philosophical point of view. Specifically this paper will aim to make plain that the reforms the current government is attempting are nothing new, nor will they succeed.

At least some of those in important positions in government are indeed the slaves of a few dead economists who, unfortunately, have been proven dead wrong by history.

Specifically, there is a real risk that the current path that some in government seem intent on following is based on flawed and potentially disastrous thinking. Thinking that has the potential to undo the positives of the past two decades and take South Africa back to a situation where the state does not act in the best interest of its people.

As a middle-aged economist with small children, I spend more time than most worrying about the longer-term prospects of the country. Perhaps actuaries spend more time in the future than macro-economists, but even they will admit to the central role that underlying economic growth, or the lack thereof, plays in any future scenario.

A chance rereading while on holiday of a literary classic from the 1930s, **The Road to Serfdom**[7], by the Austrian born, London School of Economics Professor Friedrich Hayek left me with the truly disturbing

---

[7] Serfdom relates to a condition of bondage where "peasants" were effectively controlled by higher powers typically the owners of land during feudal times. Serfs have no power to decide their own fate.

thought that nothing has changed in economics or politics. Seemingly, despite nearly eighty years having passed since the bloke wrote the book, we had learnt nothing?! Surely not?!

I freely admit to an ideological bias towards his way of thinking, but the post war era pretty much closed that specific argument for most people. While his work is by no means accepted as the gospel by all economists, the central point namely that there exists NO BETTER tool for measuring scarcity than the market, is no longer really in question. During the 1920s and well into the 1960s much thought went into trying to justify central planning, but the dismal failure of all jurisdictions where it was implemented led to the "End of History" theory by Francis Fukuyama. Fukuyama proposed an end to the debate, and argued that a Western style liberal democracy with market values will be the final form of human government[8]. Milton Friedman, writing an introduction to the 1994 edition of the Road to Serfdom, states rather unequivocally that;

"The free market is the only mechanism that has ever been discovered for achieving participatory democracy."

The market and its role in determining economic values remain central to this debate. This state of broad consensus was seemingly endorsed by our modern founding mothers and fathers at CODESA, where our constitution was negotiated and agreed upon. Somehow in the past few years things have changed in South Africa and we now regularly hear government ministers arguing for wide ranging interventions such as price control or directing, by law if needed, investment flows from pension funds towards more "socially" acceptable projects, never mind if they yield adequate returns.

While I will not be delving into the stated aims of the interventionists, it is probably safe to say that they are probably strongly influenced by socialist teachings. Much of socialism is well intentioned and often led by truly decent people who apply their own intellectual vigour to a specific problem, but probably the central most important reason that Hayek had for formulating the book dealt with how planning inevitably leads to coercion and the erosion of personal freedom.

---

[8] See Wikipedia on the topic.

Hayek argues that central planning or direction, no matter how well intentioned, leads to the erosion of personal liberty and that personal liberty is central to the efficient functioning of the market. This is something that our constitution agrees upon and for very good reason. It is important to stress that the ANC was probably the most powerful force during constitutional negotiations and agreed and subscribed to the broad principles enshrined in the constitution.

A point that will be raised several times during the course of this paper, is that the concept of a market economy and personal liberty does not imply accepting the status quo (or laissez-faire). Hayek was often accused of arguing in favour of laissez-faire which implies those with power, keep it. In the South African context this is clearly not desirable, as we have the sad and very real and visible after-effects of racial segregation and a highly skewed income and wealth distribution.

Government actions are needed to address this. Being pro-market is not the same as being pro-business. Similarly the liberal position in its true meaning does not in any way strive to maintain the privilege of some as is also often the accusation levelled in South Africa. Being a liberal does not mean being anti-government or anti-ANC at all, rather it places the emphasis on the individual as opposed to the group.

Hayek states[9]:

"The essence of the liberal position, however, is the denial of all privilege, if privilege is understood in its proper and original meaning of the state granting and protecting rights to some which are not available on equal terms to others."

Crucially, therefore, it needs to be stressed that supporting the market and personal liberty does not in any way impede the necessity of government action **in redressing** the injustices of the past. It also does not imply that privilege or the status quo of current racial and economic divides can somehow not be rectified via market neutral interventions. Government has many tools at its disposal to effect change that do not

---

[9] In the foreword to the 1956 American Paperback Edition as contained in The Collected works of FA Hayek Vol II The Road to Serfdom 2007 University of Chicago Press

necessarily detract from personal liberty or a well-functioning market. If anything a well-functioning market <u>requires</u> government intervention where the market can be seen operating sub-optimally such as in case of monopolies. Or perhaps also in the South African context to allow for more equitable access to opportunities such as education for children where historic relations might be perpetuated unless corrective measures are introduced. Hayek's work might conveniently be used by those with existing market power and better information to argue that the market must dictate and their positions left unfettered. However, a closer look at the underlying conditions required for the market to work efficiently might leave many in big business or otherwise privileged squirming with discomfort. The central point of the original liberal meaning, which Hayek supports, is that all members of society should enjoy <u>the same</u> rights and privilege. Doing so is the best way of generating sustainable economic growth and development and there are unfortunately no short cuts or panaceas.

However 'The Road to Serfdom' maps out a clear argument detailing the reason why collective and social planning advocates might, through the best intentions, pave the way for the fundamental erosion of personal liberty and freedom.

Edwin Feulner in an introduction to yet another edition of the Road to Serfdom[10] encapsulates the central message of Hayek as follows:

"Hayek employed economics to investigate the mind of man, using the knowledge he had gained to unveil the totalitarian nature of socialism and to explain how it inevitably leads to 'serfdom'. His greatest contribution lay in the discovery of a simple yet profound truth: man does not and cannot know everything, and when he acts as if he does, disaster follows. He recognized that socialism, the collectivist state, and planned economies represent the ultimate form of hubris, for those who plan them attempt – with insufficient knowledge – to redesign the nature of man… For Hayek, such presumption was not only a 'fatal conceit', but also 'the road to serfdom'."

The arguments he so eloquently makes in the book still resonate today and we South Africans ignore the warning signs at our own peril. We

---

[10] Quoted in the combined editions to the Road to Serfdom, Institute of Economic Affairs, London:UK 2005

come from an authoritarian past and we do not wish to return to one. Hayek would have argued that we are well on our way to this yet again. The book deals with several concepts and I will use the same broad structure as his book in addressing them. Obviously I am writing this in 2015, more than three quarters of a century later, and I am doing so to warn against the dangers facing modern South Africa should they follow the same path. I will constantly refer to real South African issues in my discussion. I refer to the concept of "planner" but by that I simply mean any person or group or institution that has some form of power to direct. This will include both the organisation that has the legal power to plan such as the Department of Trade and Industry (DTI), but also the so-called expert inside the DTI who makes the final decision. Even at a local municipal level you find many planners that see fit to decide on others' behalf. This obviously includes the actual town planners and also those who decide how much to tax and where to spend tax money or those that possess the power of licence for items such as taxis or liquor permits.

Many economists and other story tellers, including planners, will "find" data to support their hypotheses. Given the information overload in modern society, one can "prove" just about anything using Google… I will, simply as illustration, constantly refer to South African examples without delving too deeply into the actual policies as they are so numerous that this exercise could easily become a multi volume edition. It is truly amazing how, when I started looking for them, the examples jumped out and while there might be more appropriate examples to illustrate the pervasiveness of the interventionist mind-set in SA, it is rather startling to think that just any random day in a national newspaper contains so much that matches the criteria.

Hayek uses concepts as chapter headings and this paper will follow the same pattern. Intended for a largely non–economist audience, the chapter headings will be similar to those used in the excellent Reader's Digest Condensed Version which really brought the original book to such a mass audience.[11]

---

[11] The reader may access the original condensed version at
http://www.iea.org.uk/sites/default/files/publications/files/upldbook43pdf.pdf

4

STATE PLANNING AND STATE POWER

For the state to plan requires that the state has power to affect change in the conditions of society and the individuals who live in it but in reality the power of the state is still wielded by people only they might have other ideas about what is good for the rest of us. The success of the planners will depend on the extent to which they succeed in achieving such power therefore the very success of the process creates further incentive. A constitutional democracy such as South Africa's, provides great protection for the individual therefore any loss of personal power is by definition an erosion of personal freedom.

Hayek writes: "Many socialists have the tragic illusion that by depriving private individuals of the power they possess in an individualist system, and transferring this power to society, they thereby extinguish power. What they overlook is that by concentrating power so that it may be used in the service of a single plan, it is not merely transformed, but infinitely heightened. By uniting in the hands of some single body power formerly exercised independently by many, an amount of power is created infinitely greater than any that existed before, so much more far-reaching as almost to be different in kind." [12]

It is not a reasonable assumption or claim that the power of a central government department such as the DTI is not significantly greater than the collective power of private boards of companies. Only the decentralisation of power can reduce the absolute amount of power in society. The competitive system centred within a well-functioning market mechanism is the only system specifically designed to minimise the power of one man over another. South Africa is littered with historic examples of the coercive power of the state being used for the benefit of some but at the expense of the rest. Apartheid South Africa was filled with state planning boards that dictated what

---

[12] Ibid p40-41

could be produced and at what price. This had certain benefits to the farmers, who had more stable prices but also led to some ridiculous events like the dumping of milk during periods of over-supply of what some bureaucrat thought was the required level. The farmer made more money but nourishing milk was discarded rather than allowed to drop in price. Happy farmers but unhappy mothers and all because some nameless person thought it in our best interest…

There were also examples of groups of insiders creating exclusive groups that used the state powers to their advantage. The Broederbond is a perfect example where state patronage was often only awarded to those who were "broeders". The concept has been derided so many times as an example of the hypocrisy of the old regime but how is that different from the cronies now being allowed to charge the state extra for work done or to exclude their competitors from even competing in the first place?

While much is made of the power of corporations over their employees, it pales into insignificance when compared to real power as vested in the state. Hayek condenses as follows 'Who can seriously doubt that the power which a millionaire, who may be my employer, has over me is very much less than that which the smallest bureaucrat possesses who wields the coercive power of the state and on whose discretion it depends how I am allowed to live and work?'[13]

There is no doubt that this was true in the bad old days of apartheid, when considering laws such as influx control and the dreaded pass laws, but current examples of this type of state intervention are again all too easy to find. Look no further than the new visa regulations, which have caused such widespread harm to the domestic tourism industry and those that work in it. Or perhaps the so-called certificate-of-need that aims to regulate a more even distribution of medical doctors is a better example. The stated aim of the proposed regulation, to direct the services of private medical practitioners to areas where there is a perceived (and probably very real) need for their services, is laudable. However, the impact on the individual – who is now restricted in his/her place of work – is entirely the same in effect as

---

[13] Ibid p41

the old pass laws which restricted the freedom of movement of people based on their race group. The only difference is that race as criteria will now be replaced with skill as criteria. The proposed certificate is unlikely to be implemented due to a variety of challenges, but it highlights the type of interventions that are flouted by government. This is freely acknowledged to be a dramatisation and not intended to belittle the horrific impacts of the pass laws on people, but the principle is the same.

No matter how well intentioned, when personal liberty is eroded by the action of the state through the increase in the power of the state, the erosion of individual freedom always follows.

Hayek pulls no punches when he wrote[14]:

"It is only because the control of the means of production is divided among many people acting independently that we as individuals can decide what to do with ourselves. When all the means of production are vested in a single hand, whether it be nominally that of 'society' or that of a dictator, whoever exercises this control has complete power over us. In the hands of private individuals, what is called economic power can be an instrument of coercion, but it is never control over the whole life of a person. But when economic power is centralised as an instrument of political power it creates a degree of dependence scarcely distinguishable from slavery."

---

[14] Ibid p41-42

5

BACKGROUND TO DANGER THEN AND WHY THE CURRENT SOUTH AFRICAN DEBATE IS CONCERNING

Hayek argues that individualism, in stark contrast to socialism and other authoritarian forms of government, evolved out of the respect that modern Christianity held for the individual and the underlying belief that people should be free to develop their own destiny. This philosophy first developed fully during the Renaissance and continued to grow and spread into what we now refer to as western civilization.[15] The growth and development that was brought about during this period was brought about by the unchaining of individual energies in the field of science. Science has changed the world and it stems from the fact that everything could be attempted if somebody was willing to back a project at own risk.

Hayek states that, in 1941 already "-has science made the great strides which in the last 150 years have changed the face of the world. The result of this growth surpassed all expectations. Wherever the barriers to the free exercise of human ingenuity were removed, man became rapidly able to satisfy ever-widening ranges of desire. By the beginning of the twentieth century the working man in the Western world had reached a degree of material comfort, security and personal independence which a hundred years before had hardly seemed possible. The effect of this success was to create among men a new sense of power over their own fate, the belief in the unbounded possibilities of improving their own lot. What had been achieved came to be regarded as a secure and imperishable possession, acquired once and for all; and the rate of progress began to seem to slow. Moreover the principles which

---

[15] For an excellent explanation on the topic see David Landes' book
The Wealth and Poverty of Nations: Why Some Are So Rich and
Some So Poor 1998

had made this progress possible came to be regarded as obstacles to speedier progress, impatiently to be brushed away. It might be said that the very success of liberalism became the cause of its decline." [16]

Indeed one might argue, that the very fact Marx was allowed the freedom to develop his theories on his own in a library was as a direct result of liberal thought in practice, in that he was allowed to develop his own talents rather than being directed to work somewhere. Germany was the first to really abandon liberalism during the 1920s and "perfected" organisation or planning during the 1930s.

Initially it seemed as if the wave of socialist theory and practice would sweep all before it with its success but we all know how this ended...

Now eighty years later, the very same arguments for central direction and planning are yet again making headlines.

---

[16] http://www.iea.org.uk/sites/default/files/publications/files/upldbook43pdf.pdf p43

6

THE LIBERAL WAY OF PLANNING, OR RATHER, IS THERE SUCH A THING?

It is obviously sensible that we as a society should try and address the challenges facing us with as much thought and foresight as possible. Hayek and liberal thinking do not in any way mean that we should not employ as much systemic and rational thinking as possible in planning our affairs. However, the best way of going about this, is clearly in question here... Should we create conditions that allow for people to plan and execute their decisions themselves, or should we try and direct and organise economic activities according to a formulated plan that consciously directs the resources of society to conform to the particular views of those doing the planning?

Again quoting from the defunct economist directly[17]:

"It is important not to confuse opposition against the latter kind of planning with a dogmatic laissez faire attitude. The liberal argument does not advocate leaving things just as they are; it favours making the best possible use of the forces of competition as a means of coordinating human efforts. It is based on the conviction that, where effective competition can be created, it is a better way of guiding individual effort than any other. It emphasises that in order to make competition work beneficially a carefully thought-out legal framework is required, and that neither the past nor the existing legal rules are free from grave defects. Liberalism is opposed, however, to supplanting competition by inferior methods of guiding economic activity. And it regards competition superior not only because in most circumstances it is the most efficient known but because *it is the only method which does not require the coercive or arbitrary intervention of authority.*"

---

[17] Ibid p45

Hayek then provides several examples of types of conditions where the state may and should intervene, such as limiting total working hours and policing working conditions, or where some costs are not included in the perceived cost of manufacturing, for example pollution or deforestation, and the owner does not actually carry the costs associated with the activity. Economists call these costs externalities and they are now routinely included in analysis. However, the central point in this section is, even though the state should on occasion intervene when the conditions for the proper working of competitive forces cannot be created, it does not imply or prove that we should intervene to suppress the effects of competition where it can be made to function well. But surely this means that it must somehow be possible to find a middle ground between directing activity and allowing competitive forces? Unfortunately it is the case that both competition and central planning become inefficient if they are incomplete and therefore mixtures of the two simply do not work. They should only be combined when the intention is to plan FOR competition rather than AGAINST competition.

South Africa seems not to be taking this course at all, showing an increased desire for state intervention and control in addressing many/all of society's problems. Interventions regularly mentioned in South Africa range from granting state owned companies special privileges even though the companies might be competing with other private sector companies, or simply dictating how the private sector needs to be structured. The bailouts of state owned enterprises such as SAA, PetroSA and the Post Office, for example, have received vast media coverage but often, assistance in not limited merely to financial aid.

The state is also intending to crudely intervene in matters such as the maximum size of commercial farms. The state has indicated that there will be a hard/crude cap of say 5000ha on a farm. This does not take matters such as efficiencies of scale into consideration at all nor questions such as non-arable land like mountains. Also just practically, what if the farm is currently 5001 hectares? While the political imperative might have merit, without allowing for any scale advantages, the state might inadvertently punish those farmers who are more successful over time than others, thereby raising the final cost of production or eroding food security.

Economists will argue that one should strive for the most effective production levels i.e. at the lowest possible average cost of production. State interventions that focus solely on one aspect only, namely the size of the productive unit, simply ignore this aspect entirely. The liberal argument is that it is most appropriate to allow the market to dictate the most efficient outcomes, but that the state then extracts taxation with which to affect their agendas. This does not imply leaving the status quo as is, rather the state might preferably use its power to allow for more competition, possibly by assisting emerging farmers in improving their own competitiveness and lowering their average costs.

In other words, allow the market to function and people to maximise their incomes, THEN extract some of the surplus to assist where the political need directs. This assistance needs to be directed at improving market efficiencies rather than distorting the market. State aid in purchasing farms at the going market rate for certain groups is perfectly acceptable, as long as this is coupled with ensuring that the recipients are able to compete effectively with the established farmer next door. Giving a person a farm but without the needed experience and knowledge, tools and operating cash flow implies that the farmer will not be able to compete efficiently. By competing it is understood that the farmers must be able to compete on the same set of conditions and not where the state somehow hampers the functioning of one group to the advantage of another.

The intention of lowest cost of production MUST remain the objective rather than having the political objective supplanting the economic objective. When the objective is solely the political transfer of ownership or control, then economic efficiency will always be lost. The loss of economic efficiency harms the entire country and all the people, not only the parties directly affected. Land reform is needed in South Africa and this must surely include more demographically representative farming communities. State intervention must be based on assisting those that are excluded to successfully compete with those already present.

South Africa has a torrential volume of plans with which to address various issues facing society. Hayek is clear that as long as planning allows for MORE competition then it is acceptable, but when it lessens competitive forces for whatever reason, it should be abandoned given the costs associated.

The perceived current reality is that this is certainly not the case.

Many, if not most, actual and proposed state interventions are aimed squarely at increasing the role of the state in directing economic activity even at the cost of economic efficiency.

7

THE GREAT UTOPIAN DREAM HAS NOT REALLY CHANGED

Hayek, writing at the time of Nazism in Europe and Stalinism in Russia is understandably strong in his defence of individual liberty, but argues that many socialists believe that they are able to combine socialism and individual freedom. Yet he points out that socialism was early recognised as a grave threat to freedom and that at its inception it was frankly authoritarian[18]. Socialism came about as a reaction to the liberalism of the French Revolution, and the writers who laid the foundations for socialism had no doubt that their ideas could only be put in place by strong dictatorial government. One of the early planners, Saint-Simon, predicted that those who did not obey their planning would be 'treated like cattle' – a chilling statement when read in the context of the second world war and the persecution of peoples by both the Nazis and the Soviets.

Hayek, in his turn quoting the great political thinker de Tocqueville states[19]:

"Democracy and socialism have nothing in common but one word: equality. But notice the difference: while democracy seeks equality in liberty, socialism seeks equality in restraint and servitude."

The freedom from necessity, as opposed to freedom from coercion and the power of others that came to be associated with socialist writings, rested on the assumption that somehow planned economies would produce substantially larger outputs than their market friendly and competitive alternatives. This false hope has been so convincingly thrashed in the second half of the 20th century that it remains frankly amazing that there are still those who believe in the theory behind

---

[18] Ibid p47

[19] Ibid p47

central planning. There exists no better form of economic organisation than the market based economy that rests on the rule of law and is legitimised by means of regular, free and fair elections.

The stated aim of modern socialists and many liberals is to increase the amount of goods available for sustainable distribution to those in need; i.e. freedom from necessity in society. The best system is still a market based economy governed by a legitimate state that supports and defends the rule of law and uses a progressive tax structure to alleviate need where possible.

The struggle against apartheid was in essence the desire of people to be regarded as free and equal citizens i.e. free men and women who may not be dictated to by a coercive government on the basis of skin colour (or any other criteria). The final outcome of the constitutional negotiations that saw the birth of the modern South Africa recognised the rights of the individual as protected by the highest law in the land, namely the Bill of Rights. While class and race are clearly still important as a defining feature, the founding fathers specifically wished to elevate the individual to the top of the pyramid and limit the state's power over the freedom so dearly achieved by the people of the country.

Modern ANC thinking still allows for the theoretical supremacy of the individual. Quoting directly from the discussion paper of the ANC in 2012[20]:

"The bedrock of our political system is therefore highlighted as:

- *A legitimate state that derives its authority from the people through regular elections and popular participation.*

- *The mobilisation of the nation around a common vision of the kind of society and world we are building, acting in partnership with each sector for the realisation of the common good.*

- *The means for citizens to exercise their human rights, and for checks and balances in a law-governed society.*

---

[20] THE SECOND TRANSITION? Building a national democratic society and the balance of forces in 2012. A discussion document towards the National Policy Conference, Version 7.0 as amended by the Special NEC 27 February 2012 paragraph 57

- *Building the South African nation inclusive of the multiple identities based on class, gender, age, language, geographic location, and religion, as a united African nation, adding to the diversity and identity of the continent and humanity at large."*

Hayek argues that democratic assemblies unfortunately cannot function as planning agencies, as it is impossible to agree on what the final allocation of every conceivable resource in society should look like. In reality it is always inevitable that the task of planning to address the vague and imprecise notion of 'general welfare' is delegated to some so-called expert. This simply transfers massive power away from the people and towards some 'insiders'. The democratic assembly loses its position as the highest form of societal representation when it delegates power to institutions of state that aim to centrally direct the private activity of individual members of society. This is currently highlighted by the conflict between the sovereignty of parliamentary oversight and the role of the constitutional separation of powers in the ongoing saga between the Presidency, Parliament, the Public Protector's office, the Department of Public Works and public representatives in parliament.

Planning leads to authoritarian or dictatorial rule because a dictatorship is the most effective form of coercion and coercion is required if planning is to occur on a large (society wide) scale. There is simply no justification for the belief, hope is perhaps a better word, that as long as power is conferred by democratic means that the power cannot be arbitrary. The process of applying state sanction must be clearly defined, in other words there needs to be a set of rules that govern when and how the state is allowed to use its coercive power. The state, or any institutions within the state, must never be allowed to make up its own rules arbitrarily. Power needs to be limited so as not to become indiscriminate and this is only possible when power to coerce is limited and very clearly governed by a predetermined set of rules (also called the rule of law).

The conclusion drawn is that any so-called dictatorship of the proletariat, even if democratic in form, that wishes to centrally direct the economy, would most probably have to destroy personal freedom as completely as any of the scary experiences of pure central planning experiments such as Pol Pot's Khmer Rouge or Mao's cultural revolution phase or even Hitler's Germany.

The concept of our own "second transition" and associated needs do seem to indicate such intent from some within our current government. The wording in the discussion paper surrounding the second transition does create the impression that the governing party has accepted that the state can and must direct economic enterprise in South Africa. Again quoting directly from the paper[21]:

" We have made significant progress, but the central task in this phase is to build a developmental state that is people-centred and uniquely South African. It is thus defined as a state that leads and directs national development and mobilises society around this vision and its implementation.

A developmental state must have the technical and organisational capabilities to:-

- *intervene and direct economic development and transformation in the interest of higher levels of industrialisation and diversification, higher rates of growth and sustainable development;"*

Thus the legislative body will be reduced to choosing the persons who are able to have practically absolute power. The whole system will tend toward that kind of dictatorship in which the head of government is from time to time confirmed in his position by popular vote, but where he has all the power at his command to make certain that the vote will go in the direction that he desires.[22]

Hayek wrote the section just quoted in the early 1940s in the United Kingdom which was at war with Nazi Germany at the time, yet when reading the passage in 2015 in South Africa, it is all too easy to find chilling similarities with our current political climate. This does not in any way imply that I am drawing parallels. Highlighting the risk is the intention!

---

[21] THE SECOND TRANSITION? Building a national democratic society and the balance of forces in 2012 A discussion document towards the National Policy Conference, Version 7.0 as amended by the Special NEC 27 February 2012 paragraphs 190-191

[22] http://www.iea.org.uk/sites/default/files/publications/files/upldbook43pdf.pdf p50

As someone who saw the destruction of his own country (Hayek was Austrian) first hand, writing the following must have been a relatively painful experience:

"To those who have watched the transition from socialism to fascism at close quarters, the connection between the two systems is obvious. The realisation of the socialist programme means the destruction of freedom. Democratic socialism, the great utopia of the last few generations, is simply not achievable." [23]

As stated right at the start of this paper, economics is not called the dismal science for nothing. The risks are that a society such as South Africa might accidentally be taken down a path, possibly paved with good intentions, but that completely destroys hard won personal freedom in the long run. The state will do so without ever achieving what the original intention was, simply due to inconsistencies in the system. Hayek highlights these inconsistencies, which are proven to be insurmountable, and repeatedly warns against them. This paper will expand on them more in the sections following.

---

[23] Ibid p51

8

WHY THE WORST GET TO THE TOP IN SUCH SYSTEMS

There can be no doubt that there are differences in authoritarian systems, and it is entirely possible to get a nicer type of dictator than, for example Hitler. However, authoritarian systems typically become intolerable for freedom-loving people in the long run. For planning to work as explained, the state will need to assume more and more dictatorial powers in order to effect their plans (the alternative is to abandon them). Similarly, in time, successful implementation of plans will need to rely less on ordinary morality and more on desired outcomes. Due to this incentive (success at all cost) it is likely that those with fewer scruples will eventually be more likely to lead as they are better at implementing stated plans and objectives, i.e. the unscrupulous and manipulators are more likely to be successful in a system that relies more on planning than on individual freedoms and the market mechanism. On this point, Hayek flatly states[24]: "Who does not see this has not yet grasped the full width of the gulf which separates totalitarianism from the essentially individualistic western civilization."

Hayek then goes on to point out that many of the old school socialists were inhibited by their inherently decent and democratic ideals, and were therefore not well suited or able to deal with the inevitable challenges of implementing that which they had started.

However, there are always those that have learnt the lessons or understand the value of power sufficiently that: "in a planned society the question can no longer be on what do a majority of the people agree but what the largest single group is whose members agree sufficiently to make unified direction of all affairs possible." [25] In other words what is the minimum needed for society to hand over control of their affairs to the state.

---

[24] Ibid p51

[25] Ibid p52

Unfortunately, there are three reasons why this 'numerous' group he referred to is more likely to be formed and led by the worst elements in society rather than the best.

1. Firstly, tastes and views differ more widely the higher the level of education and intelligence of an individual, therefore the higher people reach on the human development scale the less likely they are to become part of a really homogeneous group. This is simply due to the fact that poor people must, of necessity, focus more on basic food, safety and shelter than those higher up. Once your basic needs are addressed, other diverse interests become relevant.[26] Similarly, this implies that the lower the level of education and development, the more uniform the outlook of a group of people may become and given their relative lack of knowledge, they are then also easier to control.

2. Secondly, the group might not be large enough to confer power to the leader who is seeking their support. This leads unscrupulous leaders to seek the support of the docile and the gullible in society who might have no strong conviction of their own, and are ready to accept a prepared system of values as long as it is drummed into them sufficiently loudly and frequently. *"It will be those whose vague and imperfectly formed ideas are easily swayed and whose passions and emotions are readily aroused who will thus swell the ranks of the totalitarian army."* [27]

3. Then, thirdly, to weld this group together into a closely held and coherent body of supporters, the leader can appeal to a common human weakness and agree on a negative programme or a common enemy or the envy of those better off. Hayek states this, and it is so easy to recognise in modern South Africa that the concept of 'we' and 'they' is always employed by those who seek the allegiance of the masses. The enemy identified might be internal force, like the 'Jew' in Nazi-era Germany or the 'kulak' in Russia, the 'swart gevaar' or the 'rooi gevaar' in apartheid SA or dare I say it, the white capitalist in modern South Africa. Scapegoats are easy to find and sell, especially to the less educated parts of the population.

---

[26] See Maslow's hierarchy

[27] http://www.iea.org.uk/sites/default/files/publications/files/upldbook43pdf.pdf p53

A negative programme allows the leader much greater freedom of action than any programme based on positive outlooks.

Advancement within a totalitarian grouping depends largely on a willingness of the individual to do immoral things in order to get the job done, as the end justifies the means in this line of thought. "There is literally nothing which the consistent collectivist must not be prepared to do if it serves 'the good of the whole', because that is to him the only criterion of what ought to be done." [28]

Given the concept of an end goal, it then becomes apparent that if the leader can convince the people of such, all acts to reach that goal are acceptable as they are mere instruments of policy approved by almost everybody but those who are victims of the policy itself. Frank Knight, another now defunct economist, is quoted by Hayek as noting that the authorities of a collectivist state "would have to do these things whether they wanted to or not: and the probability of the people in power being individuals who would dislike the possession and exercise of power is on a level with the probability that an extremely tender-hearted person would get the job of whipping master in a slave plantation." [29]

Truth can also not be allowed free reign in a planned or controlled society and collectivism means the end of truth in the broad sense. Hayek states this as follows:

"To make a totalitarian system function efficiently it is not enough that everybody should be forced to work for the ends selected by those in control; it is essential that the people should come to regard these ends as their own, this is brought about by propaganda and by complete control of all sources of information." In other words, the regulation of the media through whatever means, is a way for those that have and seek power to gain even more. It also becomes imperative for leadership to silence those who do not agree with them as this erodes the strength of the support that they enjoy. In this way, disagreement or uncertainty regarding the stated objectives of the state must be controlled and suppressed as they might produce results not foreseen

---

[28] Ibid p53

[29] Ibid p54

by those doing the planning. While South Africa has a laudable free press, the attacks on the freedom of expression by those holding dissenting voices has steadily grown over the past few years, and there is often open hostility between several factions in government and some holding and expressing dissenting voices. The press in South Africa has long been challenged by state power. Extensive media restrictions were the norm under the previous dispensation as were covert attempts at direct control. The SABC was often directed by the security establishment during the state of emergency as to what they were allowed to report. This led to strong opposition within the media by independent journalists and the South African media has a justifiable reputation for not being cowed by state power.

The constitution of South Africa guarantees a free press, yet the attacks on and defence of the public protector in the ongoing saga of Nkandla is a good example of how fragile this freedom truly is. It should concern all citizens that the government tried to prohibit the use of cell phones in parliament during the ongoing and controversial Nkandla saga. This not because of any particular issue with Nkandla, as opinions on this matter differ, but rather because of the fact that government was willing to go to such lengths as to scramble the cellular signal in parliament in order to restrict information shared with outside media for further distribution. It had nothing to do with Nkandla and everything to do with media freedom and the right of citizens to see what their parliamentary representatives are up to.

9

PLANNING VS THE RULE OF LAW. SURELY IT ALL DEPENDS ON THE DEFINITION?

There is nothing that more clearly defines a free country from one under arbitrary rule than the observance of a great set of guiding principles often called the rule of law. Stripped to its core this means that government in all of its actions is bound by rules fixed and agreed upon BEFOREHAND – rules that allow for the possibility of foresight in regards to the conditions under which the government is allowed to use its coercive powers in any given set of circumstances. Within these rules, the individual is free to pursue his or her personal goals, with the reasonable certainty that government will not frustrate his or her efforts.

Socialist economic planning or the developmental state, where the state becomes an actor that directs and takes part in the economy, involves the very opposite of the rule of law as it applies here, as the government will not wish to be circumscribed in its potential actions. The state cannot be impartial if the state is also an economic actor. Under planning scenarios the state ceases to be a simple utility intended to assist individuals in their fullest development or guards against abuses of power by some over others and becomes an active participant.

By the rule of law it is meant that the rules stay constant and constrain the actions of the state as well. It does not imply that the rule of law is necessarily just and equitable. There is no doubt that the apartheid government excelled at using the legal system to enforce its own agenda. By rule of law it is implied that the state may also be constrained in which actions or policies are allowed.

The state, in its active "developmental" capacity, has to deliberately discriminate between the particular needs of different groups/people. By having been granted special privilege, state institutions are allowed to do what others are prohibited from doing. This is inherently unfair to all others as the market now cannot function to determine true value, given the monopolistic nature of state institutions, as they become less the neutral referee and more the powerful actor.

"The rule of law, the absence of legal privileges of particular people designated by authority, is what safeguards that equality before the law which is the opposite of arbitrary government." [30]

It is fair to say that South Africa had a multi-decade period of struggle for a just and equitable dispensation for all – and not just some of the people. There can be no denying that the old South Africa abused the law in order to benefit the state and privileged elites. This struggle for freedom from state oppression culminated in a constitution that placed the fair and equal rule of law and supremacy of individual rights above arbitrary state power as the abuses had been noted.

The guiding principle of South Africa should be that Government can never be allowed to subvert the constitution or the freedom of any individual.

This does imply that stress between government and those tasked with protecting the rule of law is inevitable, but that the rule of law must always triumph. If this is allowed to be reversed and government subjugates the rule of law, then the erosion of personal freedom inevitably follows.

---

[30] Ibid p58

10

IS PLANNING INEVITABLE
IN ANY MODERN COUNTRY?

It will be hard to find a bureaucrat today that openly admits that planning is desirable. Rather, the answer will probably be that the common good requires that intervention is required to rectify a specific shortcoming as it is not in keeping with the aims of democracy, the will of the people or some other political reason.

Planning is regularly called by other names, such as strategic alignment or required intervention, but the intentions and end result are the same; namely central direction and control. Often planning, or government intervention, is justified by citing objectives to promote competition on a more level playing field, and that leaving things up to market forces would result in the loss of a strategic sector. Sound familiar?

Planning would be feasible if conditions were so simple that a single person, board or team of experts could effectively survey ALL the facts. Unfortunately, as things become a bit more complex and numerous, no one entity can keep track of all variables, not to mention the dynamic effect as one set of conditions change relative to another.

It is pretty obvious, after even a cursory glance at the ever-changing conditions in global and domestic trade and the demand and supply of different commodities, that the factors influencing any single transaction can never be fully known. Nor can the impacts of change be instantly calculated and the resulting implications against all other factors communicated by any one centre.

However, under competition and a functioning market, and currently under no other system, the price system automatically records all relevant data. In turn, by simply watching a few prices, market participants are able to continuously adjust their activities to those of other participants. Hayek likens the effect to an engineer who watches a few dials that reflect the most pertinent variables of a highly complex set of machinery. Compared to the nimble price mechanism, trying to direct economic activity is more like taking a crowbar to a window when needing fresh air. The ever-increasing complexity of modern society implies that our reliance and dependence on the price mechanism as signal has actually increased since the time when Hayek wrote his book. The market and price mechanism has an astounding ability to allow for the multitude of factors that affect the supply and demand for items. It does this seamlessly, if occasionally dramatically, on a continuous basis. This is highly appropriate in the ever-increasing complexity in which we live.

Unfortunately, the price mechanism is entirely automatic and devoid of any emotion, so the signal that it sends often offends people. Why is my house worth less than yours? Why is the rand so weak this year? I don't like the price of milk being so high because it means that people cannot afford it! My company pays me too little and I have nothing left at the end of the month!

The demand for a product, be it a slab of chocolate or the expertise of a brain surgeon, is determined by demand for it. There are many people that love chocolate, so the demand is very high, the market reacts and farmers across the globe plant cocoa beans. Supply increases and satisfies the demand at some point. If a new fad diet tells people to eat more chocolate, the demand increases even further and raises the price. Over time suppliers plant more cocoa and the price adjusts to a new level. Similarly, a drought reduces the supply of beans while demand stays the same and the price adjusts upwards, but this time due to a supply as opposed to demand shock. Similarly, with brain surgeons. There aren't many of them and most people will never need one, but when you do it is really urgent – i.e. the demand is extremely high and there is little supply. Bingo – high prices for brain surgery. If you want the price of brain surgery to decrease make sure there are more surgeons being trained!

But what if I just control the price of brain surgery? Unfortunately, the brain surgeon's skills are in his/her head so one might do this over the short term but eventually people go where they are able to earn more money… it is probable that some doctors are specifically attracted to neurosurgery BECAUSE of the high prices they can earn for their labour. If you now control the price at some artificial level, fewer doctors will be attracted to the specialty, thereby reducing the supply of something that is already in very short supply! Train more doctors!

The examples are clearly intended to be nothing more than illustrative, and I imagine there will be neurosurgeons – and probably our very competent minister of health – that disagree. They might blame the high costs of hospitals or the cost of pharmaceuticals used in surgery or the cost of insurance premiums and many, many other factors for the high price of their services. They are all potentially correct and this is exactly the point! There are so many variables that change constantly, that it is impossible to keep track of them all. The ONLY mechanism that is able to adjust in time is the market.

Many planners ascribe the so-called success of large corporations to scale advantage and their ability to weather short term fluctuations, but there is little or no justification for such an assumption. Big corporations also fail, and while they might have deeper pockets allowing them to weather short term storms, if they do not react to market signals they also go bust. Ask the shareholders of Lehman Brothers! Occasionally, their very size and investment in a particular technology leaves the door open for new products and companies that might disrupt the market. Ten years ago the smart phone world was dominated by Blackberry, and it was almost inconceivable that they could lose their dominance, but this is exactly what happened as they were too slow in responding to the threats from other players such as Apple and Samsung.

Large scale successful intervention by state owned enterprises in China is cited as a justification for the so-called developmental state argument in South Africa. Yet there is ample evidence that the dramatic growth of private enterprise in China very significantly outpaces those by public enterprise. Only since the start of market friendly liberalisation in China has the Chinese economy achieved the dramatic success of the past few decades.

Monopolies are inherently bad for social welfare as they extract more of the surplus through higher prices than would be the case if the market were left to settle on its own. Monopolies simply mean we all pay more than we should. It is not unreasonable to state that the majority of monopolies require collusion, in secret or otherwise, to function. Fortunately, there is a concerted and laudable effort by the Competition Commission to restrict collusive practices in South Africa given the damage they cause to consumer welfare.

Government intervention to provide market power to some participants through market direction or interference, when it is not available to all, is monopoly power by any other name. It is difficult, or even impossible, to see how a government monopoly (such as ESKOM for example) can be any better to general welfare than any other monopoly, yet somehow this is never really acknowledged or questioned, because the state entity is operating for the so-called general welfare. Government is specifically excluded from the scope of the Competition Act of 1998. In other words, government is allowed to act in ways that the rest of us are not, but they supposedly are doing so in our best interests?

Protectionist policy also provides fertile ground for the formation of monopolies, as it crudely distorts the price mechanism. So when one industry is protected against competition, not only do consumers end up paying more, but there is often a misallocation of resources in sectors that would otherwise be attractive enough were they allowed to operate on their own merit. There is no doubt that states routinely intervene in markets in order to leverage more for their respective countries. Unfortunately, intervention carries costs, either directly in terms of subsidies or indirectly due to skewed allocation of resources or punitive measures taken by other countries. The net effect is that the domestic consumer loses either by paying higher taxes in order to afford the subsidies, or through diminished market access in other countries for SA goods. The ongoing trade disputes with the USA surrounding poultry make for a perfect case study on the phenomenon of the manner in which vested interests in countries (competing poultry producers in South Africa and the USA) use state power to further their own agendas[31]. International trade policy has developed rapidly since the time of Hayek's book, and there are many market neutral remedies available to counter unfair competition, other than protectionist policies.

---

[31] For a very good interpretation see
http://www.dailymaverick.co.za/article/2015-04-20-agoa-south-africas-real-chicken-and-egg-problem/#.VdMuqLKqqko

Achieving sustainable economic growth and development does not imply that planning is inevitable. Groups such as organised capital and organised labour prefer the monopolistic organisation of industries as it increases their relative power. By organising or colluding with one another and among themselves both capital and labour are able to generate more profits for themselves. However, these higher profits (return on capital for capital and higher wages for labour) stemming from this collusion are at the expense of the broad community and particularly at the expense of those employed in less well-organised industries or the informal sector. Hayek and the original liberal traditions are completely opposed to this. South Africa has a highly organised labour movement and big capital similarly enjoys significant market power, yet both sides tend to argue for state interventions for themselves and/or other actions in the name of the broad public good or the working class. Please note that the implication is not that labour should not be organised within a federation like COSATU, or that mining companies cannot join forces in the Chamber of Mines. They must be limited in the time and manner in which they may exercise their significant powers, in ways that are predictable and do not come at the expense of another portion of society. In a society governed by the neutral and independent rule of law, they should not be able to use their market power at the cost of society. This should apply both to COSATU and the Chamber in the example equally.

11

CAN PLANNING FREE US FROM CARING ABOUT THE LESS FORTUNATE?

There is little doubt that in order for planning to work, it must be run along dictatorial lines, as the system is complex and there are so many interrelated activities that the only way to direct it efficiently would be by a team of experts that require ultimate power to direct and affect change.

A successful planner cannot be inhibited by the ebbs and flows of changing public opinion if they are to achieve their goals. Planners will try and convince us that this, frankly authoritarian view, need only apply to economic matters in society. Somehow it shall balance out when we lose some freedoms in exchange for the pursuit of higher values? This way, many people who would hate the idea of a political dictator will happily accept an economic one.

But in reality it is practically impossible to separate our political/social/family life from our economic existence.

The concept of money plays an overwhelming role in our lives, whether we like it or not. What is often referred to in a derogatory manner as 'the profit motive' is simply the rationale behind the market method that ultimately leads to the most efficient allocation of resources. Referencing open source Wikipedia, the profit motive can be described as follows:

"The profit motive ensures that resources are being allocated efficiently. For instance, Austrian economist Henry Hazlitt explains, "If there is no profit in making an article, it is a sign that the labour and capital devoted to its production are misdirected: the value of the resources that must be used up in making the article is greater than the value of the article itself."[1] In other words, profits let companies know whether an item is worth producing. Theoretically in free and competitive markets, maximizing profits ensures that resources are not wasted." [32]

A simple Wikipedia definition of economic incentive as opposed to profit is defined as thus[33]:

"The study of economics in modern societies is mostly concerned with remunerative incentives rather than moral or coercive incentives – not because the latter two are unimportant, but rather because remunerative incentives are the main form of incentives employed in the world of business, whereas moral and coercive incentives are more characteristic of the sorts of decisions studied by political science and sociology."

Money offers the widest choice in enjoying the fruits of our efforts, as once earned or possessed it grants the holder the freedom to spend it as they wish. With limited money, the restrictions that relative poverty places on the individual are highlighted through the limitation of choice. Because this can and does lead to such **glaringly obvious disparities between people, many hate money as the symbol of these restrictions.** But money is actually one of the **greatest freedoms** ever invented by man as it allows the holder access to greater choice – inherently a personal freedom.

Even if we have free choice as consumers, should production somehow be directed or controlled, we still loose freedom, as we would never know what might have been. Directing production results in the scenario where you can have any car as long as it's black, as the old saying went – referring to limited choices available when cars first became mass produced…

Freedom of choice, in a competitive society, rests on the fundamental fact that if one person refuses to satisfy our wishes, we are able to turn to another who will. If the providers are monopolists, we are left to their tender mercies. Any activity that directly controls or directs what is produced or consumed and at what price effectively strips the individual of his right to freedom of choice.

Any attempt by the state to direct the entire economic system or value

---

[32] https://en.wikipedia.org/wiki/Profit_motive accessed 18 August 2015

[33] https://en.wikipedia.org/wiki/Incentive#Economics accessed on 18 August 2015

chain is like having the most powerful monopolist imaginable, as it would have complete control over what we are given and under which terms. Now your own view of what you should have no longer matters as some nameless person decides on your behalf. Organised labour is a good example of such power, as those outside of the formal system are prevented from joining the labour force by the exercise of control over aspects such as employment policies or wage rates. Organised labour might have the best of intentions for their members, but the fact remains that they are able to keep out those who might wish to work under different conditions or rates, but are not allowed the choice of doing so.

This is an emotive topic in South Africa, sure, but yet another example of pure monopolistic power not in line with personal freedom and only to the benefit of those people who are part of the collective. The same was true for mining companies when they restricted their hiring practices or were granted special rights to recruit migrant labour more cheaply than other labour.

The point is that, whenever personal freedoms are restricted by those who decide on your behalf, the loss of personal freedom for all follows.

In a free and competitive market most, if not all things, may be had at some price, but it is often a cruelly high price as one must sacrifice one thing to afford another.

The alternative, however, is not freedom of choice, but rather the ultimate restriction of choice and freedom.

Making these hard choices that limited finances imply is difficult and people will wish that they do not need to choose at all. Unfortunately, people are only too easily convinced choice is not really necessary and that it is imposed on them merely by the set of economic conditions in which they find themselves. The "victim of circumstance", the "market" or "big business" is often told that they are not to blame, rather that they were innocent victims of a nefarious corporation or system. I refer the reader to the section on "why the worst get to the top" and how this is then manipulated by those seeking power. The devastating tragedy of Marikana has been used by various political groups to highlight their personal agendas. There is little value in denying that there was great manipulation of the situation by many and that, in general, it was about scoring political points rather than genuine concern for the situation. I am sure many will not agree with this, but it is food for thought at least.

Unfortunately, what people resent, in truth, is that there is an economic problem with infinite needs and limited resources i.e. the real world. There are poor people in Marikana, Mumbai and Memphis and the intention in economics should be to elevate as many people as possible out of poverty. For this you need growth – always.

If directed economies were able to increase output sustainably, then there might be some argument to be made for central direction and planning, but this assumption has been so clearly thrashed out in the past fifty years as to not need repeating here. They do not work. Even economies that are often cited as great examples of the success of planning, such as South Korea and Singapore, always relied on the private sector, the profit motive and free enterprise to kick-start the process. While government was very active in these countries, they typically created enabled spaces and sectors and left it to the market to grow. Singapore is a wonderful example of the manner in which government can be a tremendous partner in development. The Economic Development Board is the lead government agency for planning and executing strategies that enhance Singapore's position as a global business centre and grow the Singapore economy. It is responsible for designing and delivering solutions that create value for investors and companies in Singapore[34]. The focus is on investors and companies NOT the state i.e. they enable a better environment for the market to operate efficiently.

The Singaporean government further supported a very robust rule of law, improved education to undreamt of levels and has zero tolerance for corruption. A progressive state whose role is to improve the functioning of the market by improving education implies that citizens were constantly able to improve their own lot. I doubt you will find a Singaporean who does not value their government so there need be no trade-off between market friendly policies and state involvement, as long as the state involvement revolves around

---

[34] See https://en.wikipedia.org/wiki/Economic_Development_Board for more

improving conditions evenly. Even China's dramatic growth has been more due to the private, internationally competitive sector than any public company interventions.[35]

Modern day planners have given up on the idea of generating greater output and are now more focussed on a more equitable distribution of wealth. If we wish to consciously decide who has what, we must plan the whole economic system. But at what price? Is the price of this dream, namely equal wealth, not bound to lead to greater discontent and require more oppression than is currently the case?

It is simply irrational to expect the neurosurgeon to have equal wealth or status to a university economist such as myself. There are several thousand people with advanced economics degrees but probably no more than a few hundred neuro surgeons. The same is unfortunately true for all other forms of labour in society.

By all means allow for some minimum basic living standard if this is affordable, but then improve the ability of people to better compete in the modern world. Only true equality of all individuals can be equitable and answer the massive complexities and innumerable questions of relative merits that define a modern society.

Is it reasonable to expect equality of income between say a paediatrician and an economist? What about between a lawyer and a politician or a hairdresser and a school teacher? But what if one is black and one is white? What if both are white / black or refuse to be defined by the colour of their skin? What about sexual preferences or religion or relative wealth? Should a black teacher be remunerated better than a white teacher? What about an Indian hairdresser versus a coloured teacher? The magnitude of variables become overwhelming very soon and for this reason the best and only genuine alternative is the right of choice and freedom from arbitrary oppression of any and all individuals in society.

Greater as opposed to pure equality is surely a more laudable aim? But again this requires state largesse if the government is to affect change, and that requires a surplus to distribute. Surplus requires economic growth, and a market economy based on individual rights

---

[35] See Woetzel &Townson, 2013 The 1 Hour China Book, Towson Group LLC.

and freedoms and the rule of law is better at achieving this than all others. We are back at square one…

It is often said that political freedom is meaningless without economic freedom. True in 2015 South Africa, but Hayek made the same statement way back in 1941.[36] He goes on to say "The economic freedom which is the prerequisite of any other freedom cannot be the freedom from economic care which the socialists promise us and which can be obtained only by relieving us of the power of choice. It must be that freedom of economic activity which, together with the right of choice, carries also the risk and responsibility of that right."

So, sad as it may seem, you cannot have one without the other. You also cannot have both unless in a free society where the individual may choose his or her own destiny. Taking from one to give to another erodes the rights of both. Again you wonder why economics is called the "dismal science"?

---

[36] http://www.iea.org.uk/sites/default/files/publications/files/upldbook43pdf.pdf
p66

12

TWO KINDS OF SECURITY IN THE 21ST CENTURY

There is little doubt that many who read this piece will immediately argue that South Africa is very different from the developed world and is faced with an immense level of inequality that requires government intervention to address.

The simple fact is that this is true.

Hayek, writing at the end of the Great Depression and in the midst of the war was no stranger to the massive challenges facing his society at the time. He fully acknowledges the importance of economic security as an indispensable condition of true/real liberty and states that "independence of mind and strength of character is rarely found among those that cannot be confident that they will make their way by their own effort."[37] In other words, it is unreasonable to expect people who are not secure in their financial or economic well-being to act the same as those that are. There are two kinds of security in this respect. The certainty of a minimum level of sustenance for all is one. Secondly, the security of a given standard of living or the position of one person (or group) relative to others is another.

Hayek would wish the first level of security to be guaranteed to all but he was writing for a country (Great Britain) which at the time was very wealthy. He stated that this guarantee of a minimum of food, shelter and clothing to preserve health need NOT endanger general freedom. In a sense Hayek, when he stated that there is no reason why the state should not help to organise a "comprehensive system of social insurance in providing for the common hazards of life", could be seen as one of the original supporters of the welfare state, but he was adamant that this must not occur at the expense of individual freedom. This is not an insignificant requirement and we ignore it at our peril.

---

[37] Ibid p66

Planning for security of the second kind has an insidious effect on liberty as it depends on assumptions of what is required. It is the planning designed to protect either individuals or groups against diminished incomes that is most dangerous. This was exactly the intention of apartheid legislation in reserving certain high paying jobs in mines for whites only. These power relations became very apparent and became more enmeshed as time passed and those with power consolidated their positions.

In South Africa, the situation is currently the other way round. The intention is to bring about a transfer of wealth from the historically wealthy and privileged white population to the rest of the country, but this is a slippery slope in the extreme. The Broederbond started as a collective organisation aiming to improve the situations of poor white Afrikaners who saw themselves as marginalised by the powerful English section of the white population, and succeeded over time in becoming an exceptionally powerful force shaping events and influencing political decisions far beyond their initial intentions.

If any group, where conditions are allowed to improve like the Afrikaners, is allowed power to exclude others from their gains, those in the sectors or areas where demand has fallen off will have nowhere to go. This is probably true of organised labour in South Africa. Take, for example, the effects of higher wages in the mining sector following the protracted and mostly protected strikes of the past few years. While there is a massive reaction to the planned 2015 retrenchments of those workers no longer affordable to the mines, the impact of lessened income for the mines also led to massive job shedding in associated industries such as manufacturing.

The concept of "insiders" with regards to black economic empowerment also leads to the creation of new elites that are able to manipulate the system to their advantage NOT the advantage of those that do not directly benefit. Is the principle of having a black only management forum not perhaps the same as the Broederbond in the early days?

Any group that enjoys protection by the state and occupies sheltered positions in the economy, whether as employee at a state owned enterprise, part of unionised formal labour, a tenderpreneur/crony capitalist or the old school wealthy capitalist, will never appreciate the utter hopelessness of those excluded from this sheltered existence and the rigidity of trying to break out.

Hayek stated: "there has never been a more cruel exploitation of one class by another than that of the less fortunate members of a group of producers by the well-established. This has been made possible by the 'regulation' of competition. Few catchwords have done so much harm as the ideal of a 'stabilisation' of particular prices or wages, which, while securing the income of some, makes the position of the rest more and more precarious." In other words, the harder planners/government tries to control for adverse effects, the worse they make the situation for the rest.

If you guarantee to some a fixed part of the pie, the rest of the (unfortunately) variable pie will by definition then need to fluctuate more, increasing the uncertainty to the rest of society.

In other words by controlling some prices, whether wages or the cost of input scrap metal, the rest of the system will become more volatile as demand is unfortunately never stable. It is not a nice thing to accept, but an economic reality that cannot be escaped. It is impossible to control all prices.

Hayek's ideas, like those of many market orientated economists today, are often attacked for not caring about the conditions of the poor but it is hard not to argue that his advice of "let a uniform minimum be secured to everybody by all means; but let us admit at the same time that all claims for a privileged security of particular classes must lapse, that all excuses disappear for allowing particular groups to exclude newcomers from sharing their relative prosperity in order to maintain a special standard of their own. There can be no question that adequate security against severe privation will have to be one of our main goals of policy. But nothing is more fatal than the present fashion of intellectual leaders of extolling security at the expense of freedom. It is essential that we should re-learn frankly to face the fact that freedom can only be had at a price and that as individuals we must be prepared to make severe material sacrifices to preserve it." [38]

---

[38] Ibid p69

The above was written seventy-five years ago… heady stuff and pretty revolutionary in its implications. It is acceptable to have a caring state and tax the wealthy to pay for that care, but let them make their money in the free market first. Yet Hayek is often associated with those who prefer not to understand the actual reasoning and prefer to simply label him and his work as anti- change or pro laissez-faire[39] when nothing could be further from the truth. Hayek essentially makes the case that there should be some form of welfare state in place and that this modern requirement is not at all in conflict with the market or the rights of individuals. Similarly, newer style so-called free market liberals[40] that prefer the status quo and will let us believe that the market will sort everything out, also hail him as a hero. However, when there is unequal power in any market, there exists every justification for state intervention to correct it.

Hayek is opposed to **all** those with power, whether state or private sector, and whether on the side of labour or capital. His central point is that it is necessary to generate growth and that growth allows the state the means to sustainably improve the conditions of the country.

However, it is not possible to generate sustainable growth without absolute sovereignty of the freedom of the individual.

This freedom must be guaranteed by the independent rule of law against arbitrary use of power by the state and watched over by a free press. This was the intention when South Africa drafted its modern constitution and perhaps we need reminding of that again.

---

[39] Laissez-faire refers to the concept of leaving things as they are and that the market will correct itself over time. This is true only if there is no market power present which is only true ever in the theoretical world.

[40] The term liberal has almost no standard definition but is basically a philosophy based on liberty and equality. However there the several kinds of liberty and even an open source such as Wikipedia (https://en.wikipedia.org/wiki/Liberal) lists four main types namely CLASSICAL, CONSERVATIVE, ECONOMIC and SOCIAL so one is able to apply the label widely.

By all means use a highly progressive tax regime to distribute some portion of the surplus and to address issues of power in society but never at the expense of individual power and freedom. It follows then that in South Africa a very high tax structure on those with wealth is acceptable to improve the conditions of the historically poor and marginalised. It is not acceptable to restrict the personal rights of one set of people to the benefit of others as the distortions this brings about never result in sustainable long-term growth. Consequently the concept of black economic empowerment **as it is currently structured** and often seen as a zero sum game is not conducive to longer term sustainable growth. BEE in its current format targets specific individuals, which by definition excludes others, allowing for so-called insiders to accumulate vast wealth while having little or no impact on the average person.

There is no case to be made that BEE is not absolutely necessary to unlock the growth potential of the country. Black economic development and empowerment is required for growth, its current structure is not conducive in many respects, but this does not mean that the policy in principle is wrong at all.

Rather, the state must improve the conditions for the poorest by assisting them directly as much as state finances allow. The state must improve the relative position of those who are not able to compete well in the economy. In other words, the assistance should be directed at allowing the recipients of state assistance better options to compete. The most effective way must surely be through better education, yet our public schools very often fail dismally. The state must be a good provider of service. In other words, it is fine to extract tax from the wealthy to spend on the education of the poor to allow the poor a better chance at competing against the rest and escape their poverty. But the state must be held accountable for the manner in which they then spend the money or how they structure the aid. The whole process must be governed by the rule of law with a free press as oversight.

The emphasis is on sustainability. Therefore, a balance must be found between how much the state can extract to improve the material conditions of the poor and the inhibitions of growth and investment that tax policy implies.

The early years of the new South Africa was almost a textbook example of this way of thinking. Firstly, the new government stabilised the country's finances and, once stable, allowed the market to lead the way in growth, which led to a dramatic improvement in government finance followed by massive increases in available funds for social upliftment.

It is truly staggering to comprehend the increases over only a few years of direct support to the poorest in South Africa from the late 1990s and the impact of poverty alleviation cannot really be comprehended by those that do not suffer material shortage. It is, however, not nearly enough and needs to be increased further, but this cannot happen without growth.

In South Africa it is often not only a matter of finance. Our school system is very well funded when compared to pretty much all those we can compare to. However, the money often does not equate to value. School books are bought and paid for but never delivered in some areas. Children do not have working toilets or electricity in schools even though it has been budgeted for. By denying children the right to proper education, the people tasked with service delivery or the delivery of books are essentially denying those children fundamental constitutional rights!

If South Africa truly believed in equal rights with responsibility and had a well-functioning rule of law, then those responsible would be held accountable. The minister would then welcome the free press in exposing the abuse, instruct the police to arrest those responsible and ensure speedy prosecution while at the same time allowing another service provider to do the work at the correct market price... alas this is not the case and our kids go without books.

Understanding this implies that the argument is not being made for a minimalist state such as so called free-market supporters (and those with historic wealth) might wish for, as market failures which need addressing do exist in South Africa – possibly even more so than in most countries.

13

FINAL COMMENTS

This little book is not anti-government/ANC or pro any other party. The improvement made to the lives of many South Africans since 1994 is clear and this success can be credited to the ANC government. The argument is simply a rational one. There are good and bad ways of generating growth, and we as a country initially seemed to understand the conditions needed and the resultant tools they would bring to alleviate poverty. The ANC was the dominant negotiator at CODESA and was instrumental in accepting the supremacy of individual rights contained in our great constitution. There are many within the governing party that will agree with the broad arguments set out here.

Lately, however, the signs are pointing down a more familiar historical path, namely that of central planning and direction. Much is no doubt well-intentioned, but the result will be the same as has been predicted many times before.

There is little doubt in the minds of most people across racial, wealth and class structures that the state is not spending tax money efficiently due to either incapacity or lack of will. The arguments set out here show that this state of affairs is utterly predictable. The downward spiral that results from this typically leads to even more fruitless and self-reinforcing attempts at fixing the situation by force and even more planning. We will grind the economy to a halt through nothing more than our good intentions.

Eventually some existential crisis[41], either social like the Arab-spring, or economic like soviet Russia, will impact the country with all the unknown risks this entails. South Africa is running out of time but we have not done so yet!

It is required that we fundamentally accept the following: if the aim is to create a world of free men and women, only a policy of freedom of the individual can achieve the goal.

ABOUT THE AUTHOR

Cobus Venter is a senior consulting economist at the Bureau for Economic Research at Stellenbosch University where he heads up the macro services and ad hoc research division. Prior to working for the university he worked as an independent consulting economist and was also an executive director at the leading regulatory specialist consulting firm ECONEX. During his time as an economist he has consulted widely across just about all sectors of the South African economy. He has worked in various fields in the private sector, mostly as a self-employed entrepreneur, but spent more than a decade in the hotel and property trade. He is a director of Happimo.org which is described as a non-profit organisation dedicated to giving all South Africans, rich or poor, access to cutting-edge technology that can help them live safer, healthier and smarter lives. His favorite pastime is watching the growing success of Project Isizwe which delivers free WiFi to millions of South Africans so that they are better able to make informed decisions about their lives... and a bit of fishing.

He re-joined the economics profession in 2008 just in time for the great financial crisis and has been trying to make sense of the world and the country ever since. He grew up in Johannesburg but now lives in Stellenbosch with his wife and three young sons.

---

[41] The market will go through cyclical rather than existential crises, but will always settle again.